Healthy Choices
Healthy Voices

Phylicia Hollis

DEDICATION

I dedicate this book to my students.
Without you, none of this would be possible.

CONTENTS

CONTENTS

ACKNOWLEDGMENTS

I would like to thank God, my heavenly Father, for entrusting me with the tools to educate and impart knowledge to other singers and musicians. I would also like to thank my Grandparents, Mr. and Mrs. T.J. Massey for being the visionaries of this project. To my parents, Frank Hollis and Beverly Hollis, for allowing me to chase my dreams. My sister, Faith for being the voice of an educator. Breyannah Tillman, thank you for your part in editing and helping me complete this project. I am thankful for each student and family that I have ever worked with. Special thanks to my dear readers for taking out the time to invest and pursue a healthier voice.

INTRODUCTION

I have never been skinny, in fact, I have always struggled with my weight. To this day, I still have a very difficult time yielding to the temptation of eating chocolate! Yes, chocolate! After being overweight almost my entire life, I decided that I no longer wanted to be labeled as such. When I began to make healthier choices, it changed my life and MY VOICE!

I have been a singer for many years,

but what I didn't understand was that everything I was doing ultimately affected my singing. I had inconsistencies in every area of my life. My life included: inconsistent practice sessions, followed by poor eating habits, and inconsistent performances. I would go days sometimes weeks without practicing. I rarely ever exercised, and I would eat whatever I wanted whenever I wanted. As a result, I sounded awful more times than I sounded good. Who knew these inconsistencies with my voice could have been prevented by simply making healthier choices! Now am I telling you to go on a diet? Maybe. That is up to you, I just know what changing a few eating habits did for my singing voice.

When I first began teaching, many of my students desired to sing like me. They would ask, things like "Can you teach me to sing like you?" or "How can I sound like you?" My response was always that we all have our own unique voice; you will not sound like me, but you will sound like you. It wasn't until I was given the task of helping a "not so talented singer" sound "talented" that I realized every singer has the ability to make choices that will really determine his or her vocal capabilities.

As a professional vocal coach, I help singers work toward achieving a good sound. I teach all genres of music, and while I cannot guarantee each singer an award winning voice once leaving my studio or reading this book, I can guarantee increased knowledge about how your lifestyle and the choices you make can ultimately affect your singing voice.

Over my years of teaching, I have developed a theory that singing is not just with the mouth and the throat, but it requires the entire body. Think about it. The word sing is a verb; therefore, sing-ing requires ACTION! Yes, that's right! ACTION is needed when singing!

I have worked with many singers who desire to change their singing voice, but make no effort in putting my singing principles to work. These singers are not action oriented, yet they desire to see a rapid change in how they sound. In order to be an effective and successful singer, you must be committed to doing the work. While many singers sing effortlessly and with ease, there is real work taking place.

So what if I told you that you can choose how you sound? Yes, you get a choice! Would you believe me? There are choices you can make that will determine how far you go as a singer. Almost everything you do with your body will affect the voice. My theory is: Singing is breathing, hearing, and thinking. Healthy choices make healthy voices.

2: IT DOESN'T HAPPEN OVERNIGHT

We live in what is known as the microwave age. Cheeseburgers can be made in less than 60 seconds. We have very little patience, but we desire quality results. Unfortunately, these microwave and drive-thru window expectations do not work when dealing with the singing voice.

I wish I could say that people are just born with nice beautiful voices, but that is untrue. I have worked with singers and musicians of all ages, and while many of them are very talented, there is always room for growth. I have witnessed many of my younger students flourish into wonderful singers, because children and teens sometimes understand better than adults that "It Doesn't Happen Overnight."

For example, Lauren, a high school student of mine, did everything I told her to do, dieting included, and her voice literally transformed in a matter of months. She even went to the extent of juicing to get her voice up to par. This particular student came to me twice a week preparing for a college audition. During our time together she not only increased her vocal range, but she also learned how to sing runs, and was accepted into the college of her choice. I really had my hands tied with Lauren, because college auditions can be tricky. However, I am pleased to say that she received a full scholarship into the music program of her choice. Lauren accepted my theory that "It Doesn't Happen Overnight," and reached her goals.

In contrast, Andrew, an adult student of mine, was the complete opposite of Lauren. When I met Andrew, he had just received the opportunity of a lifetime to record as a background vocalist with a major recording artist. Before recording, he contacted me to take a few vocal lessons. I provided him with the same opportunities as Lauren, but he simply would not comply with any of my tips or suggestions. Unfortunately, Andrew was replaced, and did not sing on that project.

What is the difference between these two students? I'm glad you asked! The answer is simple. One was serious, and the other was not. One understood the process and the other did not. One made healthy choices and the other did not!

Singing is a process. Just like a body builder lifts weights to prepare for a body building contest, singers should consistently do vocal warm-ups and other things to prepare for performances. When a singer comes to me and says they don't sing as much, and their voice has changed, normally I can easily assess the problem after a brief interview.

It is not good for a singer to go without singing for months at a time. "If you don't use it you will lose it," is what my parents would always remind me when I would opt out of using my musical talents. While this theory should not be taken literal, there is truth in the fact that not using your singing voice over time will eventually show up in your singing. In contrast, overusing your voice also has its negative effects as well.

The voice is an instrument. When I was in grade school I played the viola.

Before playing my viola I was required to tune it, and warm-up. Likewise, before singing, one should warm-up to make sure the vocal instrument is in good shape.

Successful singers understand that they need a consistent singing regimen. When I was younger I did not have a consistent singing regimen, and it showed every time I sang. Singing once or twice a month is not a consistent regimen for someone who is considered to be a singer. If you are currently only singing once or twice a month, and it is in your shower, you are more than likely just singing for a hobby. While I encourage hobby singing, this book is for the singers that are ready to get serious about taking their voice to the next level. Singing on a consistent basis and understanding that it doesn't happen overnight is the healthy choice for a singer.

Practice Makes Improvement

"Practice Makes Perfect" is one of the most commonly overused phrases when it comes to the arts. People will lead you to believe that you must not be practicing enough if you still cannot reach that high note like you could ten years ago. Nowadays, society has coined a new phrase that puts even more pressure on us singers: "Perfect practice makes a perfect performance." However, my own personal theory is that "Practice only makes improvement."

While working on my Master's in

Education, I took a class called Developmental Psychology. I learned a lot about childhood development, and the fact that not all children will learn at the same pace. There is a chronological age, and a developmental age. There are teachable moments, and no matter how old a child is there are some things he or she will not learn until they are ready. Likewise, I use the same principles in vocal coaching. So it would be safe to say that some notes your voice will not reach until it is ready! All singers are simply not on the same level, and you cannot compare yourself to those that may be a little more advanced in their craft. I will discuss this later on, but comparison is a very unhealthy choice when trying to develop as a singer.

Restated, singing better does not happen overnight. Since everyone is not on the same singing level, we can also conclude that most of your practice sessions will not be perfect either. Practice time is the time for you to mess up. Practice time is the time for your voice to crack. You need adequate practice time before any performance.

You may not be the best singer, but I have a belief that all people can sing. Yes, I said it! All people can sing! Some may sound better than others, but we can all sing to a certain degree. Unfortunately, many singers will never reach their full potential because they do not know what their voice is capable of.

They never take the appropriate measures or even challenge themselves vocally. These singers never practice, and have no desire to take their singing to the next level. Unfortunately, if there is never a challenge your voice will remain the same, and never change.

The Challenge

So you may be wondering, how do I challenge myself vocally? I'm glad you asked. Develop a practice regimen. In developing a practice regimen, you need to make sure it is conducive to your schedule. Some singers only have time to practice once or twice a week. Some have more time. Whatever you do, you have to make time to practice.

I meet singers all the time that

admit to never practicing, and that's ok, as long as you are ok with being mediocre. You may not desire to be a good singer, but you do have the capability. You have a choice. You can choose to take your practice time seriously, or you can choose to not practice at all and remain where you are.

If you are reading this, you obviously desire to see some change in your voice. The healthy choice to pursuing a change in your voice is to simply challenge yourself to practice, if you do not practice already. It does not have to be a long drawn out practice, but you at least have to start. Your voice may crack a little, but at least you gave it a shot. Your pursuit to vocal

change was just initiated by the
challenge to practice, because practice
does make IMPROVEMENT!

3: HEALTHY PRACTICE

As I stated in the introduction, singing is hearing. If you have never heard yourself sing, you do not know what you sound like. Your voice has an identity. You should get to know your voice like the back of your hand. So, the first thing you are going to want to do is record yourself singing.

Many people hate hearing their own voice, myself included; however, knowing your own voice is a must when working toward becoming a successful singer. If you are an inexperienced singer, I recommend you start off recording yourself singing a few words, then nursery rhymes and short phrases before tackling full songs. Once you have recorded yourself and listened to how you sound, you are closer to understanding your true vocal identity. On my worst vocal days I know what notes I can and cannot reach. This is how familiar you must be with your voice.

Perhaps you are already a singer, and you already know what your voice is capable of. You are on a good track. I recommend that all singers record themselves singing on a regular basis.

It does not matter if you record audio or video of yourself. Listening to your own singing is a never-ending process. Our voices change over time, and you need a record of those changes.

The Practice Regimen

All singers need practice. If you are a singer, and you only practice once or twice a month, you need to develop a more consistent practice regimen. This excludes those of you who may be on vocal rest due to medical conditions.

I am a vocal coach, and I practice. My vocal coaches in college all practiced, so what makes you exempt? Beginner and intermediate level singers should start off practicing every 2-3 days and increase the days based on the level of advancement. More advanced and professional singers should practice every other day. I encourage all singers to have rest days especially after intense performances or vocal recording sessions.

If you want to have an extended vocal career, you will need a designated rest day. A rest day is meant to give your voice time to restore itself. If you never rest your voice, it will definitely begin to show. I recommend at least one day per week where you do not partake in any singing or loud talking. Likewise, if you have a family and children, you will have to use your voice, but please do consider your volume. You should not practice on your designated rest day.

I have challenged you to develop a consistent practice regimen, and now I am going to tell you what it should consist of.

Here is the 30-minute practice regimen I use for my students (the times and exercises can be adjusted to fit your lifestyle):

1. Physical Warm-Up (2 Minutes)

   - Stretches or Short Cardio

2. Breathing Exercises (3 Minutes)

   - Breathe in, hold your breath for 10 counts, Hiss out, Repeat

3. Vocal Warm-Ups (10 Minutes)

- This will vary based on your voice. Begin with lip trills, then advance using the vowel sounds ee, ay, ah, oh, oo. Feel free to do warm-ups you may already know, or visit www.phyliciahollisstudios. com to purchase vocal warm-ups.

4. Repertoire (12 Minutes)

- Use a song that will incorporate everything you did during the vocal warm-ups. If you are unaware of what to sing, you can start with perfecting something simple like "My Country

Tis of Thee" or "The Itsy Bitsy Spider."

5. Cool Down (3 Minutes)

- Stretches and lip trills.

Please remember, you can visit my website at www.phyliciahollistudios.com for more information, and to purchase the vocal warmups.

It is a healthy choice to develop a consistent practice regimen. If you have not already developed a practice regimen, you should develop one very soon. Your performance will always be a reflection of your private practice time. Many times singers have told me they will have it for the performance, as if some magical thing was going to happen. However, very rarely have I worked with singers that have a terrible practice regimen and great performances. You will more than likely always perform to your degree of preparation.

4: HEALTHY HABITS

Many of you have heard the phrase "You are what you eat." This phrase does not exclude singers. One thing you want to remember is that the vocal cords cannot be seen from outside the body. For this reason, as a singer you should be very careful about what you put inside your body. For example, if you are dehydrated, it will ultimately reflect in your voice.

Many singers make very unhealthy choices that have a negative effect on their singing voice. For example, I know many singers that smoke while singing or in between vocal recording sessions. Besides the Surgeon Generals' warning on the side of a pack of cigarettes, this is not a healthy practice for any singer that would like to achieve life-long success. Smoking and being in smoky areas is not healthy for the voice. I have witnessed instances where record labels have dropped artists because of similar issues. If you are a singer and you currently deal with this type of habit, my advice is to seek help immediately. Your career is at stake, and so is your voice.

Jacob was another student of mine who had a very promising career in music. Jacob, was a very heavy smoker, and I explained to him some of the risks behind his habit. When he was asked to sing at an event that could have changed his career, his voice simply would not work that day. He is still a great singer, but that ended up being one of the most shameful and embarrassing experiences for him.

Likewise, a singer's food and drink choices are also very important. I briefly spoke about my own battle with being overweight at the beginning of this book. I am by no means making this up, but I began to see significant changes in my voice once I began to make healthier food choices. I have also noticed that singers who take extra health precautions sound better, and advance quicker than those who do not.

I am not trying to put singers on a diet; however, I have noticed that those with good eating habits progress at a much quicker rate than those who do not. I encourage all singers to make healthy eating choices, because it will ultimately affect the voice.

Here are some healthy lifestyle habits I encourage singers to adapt:

- Minimum 7-8 hours of sleep per night
    - I understand that many singers have nighttime gigs, as well as full time careers. Planning ahead will help you

maintain good sleeping habits. Restated, you need to give your voice time to rest and replenish.

- Drink Plenty of Water
  - I recommend that you drink half your body weight in ounces. For example, if you weigh 180 pounds, you need to drink at least 90 ounces of water per day. The more you weigh, the more water you will need to get the most out of your voice. This does not mean you cannot drink juice and other beverages; however, I recommend water in its purest state for the best results.

- Eat Fruits and Vegetables
  - o I do not recommend heavy eating before singing because it can affect your breathing patterns. However, I do recommend a well-balanced diet that includes fruits and vegetables to keep your voice healthy and strong. Eating foods in the most natural state will help the voice in the long run. If you suffer from Acid Reflux, Kidney Disease, or Diabetes (Type 1 or Type 2), you should be very mindful of the foods you eat especially before singing.

- Exercise
  - Believe it or not, exercise is not only good for weight control, but it also helps with your breathing. If you tend to have breathing issues a lot while singing, you may want to develop a consistent exercise regimen.
- Speak at an Appropriate Volume
  - As a singer, you must protect your voice. Instead of yelling, you should use your indoor voice. I understand that many singers are into sports or activities that may call for loud talking, but remember what this could potentially do

to your voice. Consistent yelling causes wear and tear on the vocal cords over time. Also, keep in mind that whispering does more harm to your voice than help. Whispering causes you to over work your vocal cords because you are trying to be quiet. I recommend speaking at a normal volume to prevent future vocal problems.

- Practice Breathing Exercises
  - Breathing is a major part of singing. It should not be taken lightly. In order to see improvement with your voice, I recommend that all

singers practice breathing exercises.

- Develop a Consistent Practice Regimen
  - All singers need practice. Your performance will be a reflection of your practice. Develop a weekly schedule of the days you plan to practice, how long you will practice, and what you will practice.

Here are some lifestyle habits I encourage singers to avoid:

- Smoking
  - Besides the Surgeon Generals' warning, people who smoke are at a higher

risk of developing throat
cancer than those who do
not. So does it matter what
you smoke? I have debated
this question with many
students. Simply put, as a
singer, smoking or exposing
yourself to smoky
environments is simply not a
healthy choice, if you plan to
have a life-long singing
career.

- Drinking Alcohol
  - Alcohol causes dehydration.
    As a singer, you need to
    stay hydrated to get the
    most out of your voice.
- Drugs

- ○ Drugs, other than those prescribed by your doctor put you at risk for many potential losses, including the loss of your voice. If you are a singer, or know a singer that struggles with a drug addiction, please seek help immediately. There are also several over the counter prescription drugs that I do not recommend singers use. Some prescribed medication can cause dehydration. Please check with your doctor or pharmacist for the side effects of any medication you must take.
- Ice Water

- o I recommend that singers drink room temperature water. There is nothing wrong with drinking ice water; however, ice can numb the vocal cords. Numbing the vocal cords could possibly make it more difficult to sing certain notes. I have coached many students that are health experts about certain types of water; however, I do not endorse any particular brand or type, it's whatever floats your boat.

- Ice Cream and Dairy Based Products

- ○ If you are lactose intolerant, it may be pretty obvious why you would want to avoid these types of foods before singing. Ice cream and dairy based products also create unwanted mucus which will make it more difficult to sing.
- Overeating
  - ○ Overeating before you sing will affect your breathing. If you have a full stomach, it will be very difficult to breathe properly as well as sing without belching. I recommend not eating 60-minutes before a performance, unless you have a health condition

where it is absolutely
necessary to eat.

- Lots of Fried Foods
  - Fried foods also cause the body to create extra mucus. Fried foods may be a hard one to give up, but I would definitely recommend not eating fried foods within a 12-hour window before performing.
- Spicy Foods (Hot Wings, Hot Chips, Etc.)
  - Spicy foods can trigger heartburn. Heartburn or acid reflux disease is not something you want to deal with before a major performance. If you know

you have acid reflux disease, please be mindful of what you eat during the time window before your performance. Here are a few other foods and drinks that are known to trigger acid reflux disease: onions, tomato based products, orange juice, coffee, chocolate, wine, carbonated drinks, caffeinated beverages.

- Clearing the throat
  - Excessive clearing of the throat can cause hoarseness. If you are constantly feeling the need to clear your throat, please

consider seeing a healthcare professional.

- Caffeinated Beverages
  - Caffeine can cause dehydration. If you must have your daily dose of caffeinated coffee or tea remember that you should continue to drink water to stay hydrated.
- Peppermints
  - Many singers are allergic to peppermint oil. The allergic reactions can include but are not limited to tightness in the throat, excessive amounts of mucus, and frequent clearing of the throat. If you must have a piece of candy

before singing please
consider herbal or sugar free
throat lozenges.

Having suggested these things, I
can only tell you what has worked for
me and my clients. I am not a
healthcare professional, nor am I trying
to force you to give up your favorite
foods or current practices. I already told
you I have a thing for chocolate. You
can still eat ice cream, but I would not
recommend eating it before you sing.
You probably would not want to eat it
the week of a major performance either,
but you can still eat it at some point.

I also understand that many
singers make poor choices and never
experience any voice problems. I think
that is wonderful. However, I have

noticed that singers who are very intentional with their food choices excel at a quicker pace, and have more longevity in their voice. They can sing for hours and never get tired.

When training for upcoming shows, and recording sessions, I encourage all singers I work with to adopt these healthy choices, and it always works. Whether you're preparing for a talent show, beauty pageant, or even recording an album, a few minor lifestyle adjustments could save your life and your voice. Healthy choices lay the foundation for a healthier you and a healthier voice.

Normally after extended periods of singing, many singers experience hoarseness and vocal fatigue. In the event that you experience these vocal problems for greater than 3 days you will want to see a doctor. Normally a singer can recover from vocal fatigue quickly when drinking plenty of water, and resting after a big performance. However, if it takes weeks or even months for you to recover, there may be another issue. If this happens you will need to see a healthcare professional.

I also advise singers to be careful when consuming over the counter prescription drugs for allergies and the common cold. If there is a pharmacist available, please speak with them before consuming medication that could worsen your condition.

5: HEALTHY PERFORMANCE

Let's be honest, some performances just suck. This does not discount your ability to sing, it just wasn't your best performance.

Once you have learned your vocal identity (how your voice sounds), and understand what it is like to have a real practice regimen, you will have more control over your voice. All singers need some level of control over their voice. Otherwise you will end up singing all over the place. Once you gain control of your voice, even your worst performances are not so bad.

You Need a Repertoire

Having a repertoire is a healthy choice. A repertoire is simply a list or set of songs that you know. People will often call and ask me to teach them a particular song. To clarify, there is a huge difference between having a repertoire and just singing songs. Vocal coaches really do not teach songs, but they help train voices. Normally singers will learn most songs on their own, and they should. I highly encourage self-learning.

Singing full songs is really the

bonus part of a vocal coaching session. The warm-ups you practice will help you sing effectively. The purpose of a singing repertoire is to implement those daily practice warm-ups into a song. It makes no sense to practice breathing for 30 minutes if you are never going to practice the breathing while you actually sing. Everything you do in the warm-ups, from breathing to diction will be reinforced in the songs you sing.

Everyone should know a few songs, but if you are going to pursue singing as a career or even just for fun, you definitely need to "know" some songs. All singers should have perfected a few songs from beginning to end.   This means knowing the words, and the correct melody of a song before you perform it.

Choosing the Right Songs

Before you can truly focus on repertoire building, you need to know what type of songs you will be singing. I have heard many singers say things like: "I can sing anything." This may very well be true, but your voice cannot be marketed in every single market. Everyone needs a niche market. You need a repertoire that is a reflection of this niche.

To discover your niche market, you can see what types of people are in your crowd of supporters already. Remember, these are the people that will invite you to sing places, and eventually purchase your music, if you are a recording artist or plan to record.

I ask all aspiring singers and recording artists that I work with to have a "related artist" in mind. You need to be honest and ask yourself, "Who do I sound like?" Only then can you classify your voice with a specific genre. This will also help you identify your niche market and identify what type of songs you should be singing.

Many people will say things like: "I sound like myself." However, this is a very inaccurate answer for anyone that is considering going into the music business as an artist. Although all voices are different, everybody sounds like somebody. If you are a beginning singer it may be a little bit harder to classify your voice, but try your best to have at least three related artists in mind. Once you figure out "who you sound like," you will have better success at choosing songs that are appropriate for you and your vocal range. Just try not to choose a related artist that is too far from your sound.

This is not to say that you can never sing songs by anyone other than your "related artist." You are free to sing the songs of whomever you would like. This just helps singers develop a repertoire and get a basis of what they can achieve vocally.

Needless to say, I cannot count how many times I have witnessed singer's sing outside their vocal range.

You do not want this to be you! As a singer, you are not confined to the original key a song was written in. In order to protect your voice, it is ok to take a song down a key or two, or even raise the key of a song if it's too low for you. Choosing the right key for your voice will also help you in the long run.

Likewise, not all musicians can make last minute adjustments when accompanying you. You should plan in advance if you have live music. If you are singing to an accompaniment track, you also have the option of raising or lowering the key. Some accompaniment tracks come with high and low key options, others you will have to transpose yourself.

I recommend all singers have some basic knowledge of using production software such as Garageband, Logic, or ProTools in the event that you need to transpose your own accompaniment track. You do not have to know how to play or produce whole songs, but you should be aware of the very basics. You can find free tutorial videos on YouTube about transposing a song key. Or you can find people in your music community to do these things for you.

Training Ground

Singers not only need to know songs, but they need to sing them in a public setting. If you desire to sing publicly or become a recording artist, you will need some type of training ground. Simply put, in order to improve your performances, you need an audience. I cannot emphasize this enough.

I meet proclaimed singers all the time who say they haven't sung in front of an audience in 2-3 years. A professional singer simply does not go 2-3 years without singing unless they are retired, or have a major health issue.

I encourage singers that are serious about their craft to become zealous about what they do. Check social media or your local newspaper for more opportunities to sing places. If you are unable to find anything in your local city or town, perhaps you should just gather a few family members or friends after dinner one day and sing 2-3 songs in front of them. You have to start somewhere. I also encourage singers to keep a video portfolio of past performances. This will provide a visual reference for things that can be improved for the future.

I recommend the following places as training ground for singers that wish to enhance their performance technique:

- Talent Shows
- Beauty Pageants
- Weddings
- Funerals
- Choirs (Church, School, or Community Ensembles)
- Church Groups
- Family Reunions

- Karaoke
- Restaurants with Live Music
- Community Singing Groups, Etc.

There are so many places great singers flourish; you just have to find the right place for you, and your voice. As a singer you cannot afford to be afraid. You cannot be afraid of failure, rejection, or even the people that will say you cannot sing or should not be singing. You will need to understand that none of these things determine your vocal ability. You do. Consistent performance is a healthy choice for singers. After all, you don't want to be that singer that only sings once a year. With that being said, get up and go sing somewhere!

If you are trying to succeed as a singer, and you currently do not sing anywhere on a regular basis, I recommend you check out some of the places I mentioned. Also, join music organizations in your community. Once you have been singing a while, people will begin to know who you are, and they will need to know that you can at least make it through a full song. Most of all, you need to know for yourself that you can make it through a full song.

6: GETTING BETTER

People ask me all the time how do I get it right all the time. Well the answer is simple, I don't get it right all the time. As I previously mentioned, you want to be so good at controlling your voice that even your mistakes sound half way decent.

Earlier, I stated my theory that singing is: breathing, hearing, and thinking. One of the best things you can do for yourself, as a singer is to simply think. You do not have to overthink, but just think about where you are going while you sing.

A lack of direction and focus is very clear to me when I hear beginner voices. They just sing with no intent. There is no focus, and no clarity. You want to sing intentionally. Living unintentionally is not healthy; likewise, neither is singing unintentionally. You need to know where you are going. You are the only one who can determine whether or not you will get better at singing.

I know there will be times when a particular riff or run may not have been planned, but you should still have a plan. Singers who have no plan for the songs they sing will often do things like start too high, too low, or even too strong.

When you think before you sing, you are able to relax and have a plan before blurting out wrong notes. Overtime, as you advance as a singer, your thinking skills will become stronger. For example, I do not have to write down a plan for every song I sing. I teach singers I work with, that after a while, some things will come naturally. This does not mean you have stopped thinking, it just means you have more control over your singing voice. Singing should become a part of your muscle memory. Likewise, it can only come natural to you if you are taking the necessary steps to become a better singer.

One of the best ways to "Get Better" is to be around people who are better than you. Millionaires are surrounded with other millionaires. Therefore, the same principle applies to singers. If you only surround yourself with singers on the same singing level as you, you will more than likely continue to sound the same. I advise singers to get around singers that can sing better than them. Get around people that sing notes you cannot sing right now. Listen to singers that sing the type of music you want to sing. I believe in versatility; however, if you plan to sing Jazz, you should be studying Jazz singers. In order to get better, you will need to shadow singers with similar singing styles as your own. Remember I said earlier to stay close to your niche!

7: THE BENEFITS OF VOCAL LESSONS

According to my parents I have been singing since I was three years old. I had my first professional piano lesson at the age of 6, and my first vocal lesson followed a few years later. While in college, studying with my vocal coach grew my voice tremendously. I was finally able to sing notes I could never sing. Although I cannot guarantee you a brand new voice, there are many benefits to receiving vocal lessons.

If you are a singer, and you desire to become better, I recommend singing lessons. Professional athletes have trainers, and recording artists have vocal coaches. They are professionals. What is stopping you from pursuing the advice from a professional? While there are things we can achieve on our own vocally, sometimes we need extra help.

Likewise, you can't just take one vocal coaching session and expect a supernatural change. Think about it, Olympians train for the Olympics years in advance. Some things take time, but you have to be willing to commit to what your coach may be asking of you. If you are unsure about how to find a vocal coach, simply ask around in your music community, or call your local music store. You can also look online. You will want to choose someone who specializes in the art of coaching. Remember just because a person can sing really well, that alone does not qualify them to coach you.

Here are a few benefits from receiving vocal coaching:

- More Confidence
- Lower Stress Levels
- Reduced Risk of Hearing and Memory Loss
- Fewer Missed Notes When Singing
- Longevity of the Voice

- Increased Vocal Range
- Increased Vocal Health
- Increased Overall Quality of Life

I'm sure there are many more benefits that I did not list about vocal lessons, but these are some I have personally witnessed for myself, and my personal clients. Remember pursuing professional help is indeed a healthy choice! Just ask the professionals!

8: FREQUENTLY ASKED QUESTIONS

How do I prevent hoarseness after I sing?

Consistent hoarseness is normally caused from over singing or over using the voice. You will need to evaluate how often you use your voice. Do you yell often or talk loud? Do you sing notes beyond your singing range? Your breathing technique, microphone volume, or environment could also be a cause of hoarseness. When you are not required to sing or talk, you should rest

your voice. Are you dehydrated?
Sometimes you may not be hoarse, you
could very well be suffering from
dehydration. Remember, if you are
hoarse for longer than 3 days and you
are not sick you will want to consider
seeing a medical professional.

Should I use throat sprays?

I am not a licensed physician;
however, throat sprays have a tendency
to numb the vocal cords. In numbing
the vocal cords, you are doing yourself
an injustice, and will probably end up
hoarse, or with other serious throat
problems.

I have a child that sings, what is a good
age to begin vocal lessons?

Based off my personal studio experiences with young voices, I would not recommend vocal coaching for a child under the age of 7. While I have coached children as young as 4 to sing solos and have successful performances, vocal coaching requires a different level of discipline. If you have a child that is musically inclined and they are under the age of 7, I would recommend you allow them to take piano lessons until they are ready for vocal lessons. Remember, just because a child "likes singing" does not mean they are ready for one on one coaching. In the meantime, you should continue to expose the child to music, or allow them to join a children's choir or ensemble.

I am already a singer; do I need vocal

lessons?

Vocal lessons are very much so beneficial to those who can sing. I advise anyone who is pursuing a professional singing career to take professional vocal lessons if they are serious about getting better. Almost all professional singers have vocal coaches, why shouldn't you?

For other questions, comments, and concerns, please email info@phyliciahollisstudios.com. I look forward to hearing from you!

ABOUT THE AUTHOR

Phylicia Hollis is a well sought after piano teacher
and vocal coach. As the owner of Phylicia Hollis
Studios, in Memphis, TN she has educated
hundreds of singers and musicians from ages 3 to
80. As a professionally trained musician and singer
Phylicia has traveled to Germany, Austria, Belgium,
and Luxembourg with groups such as The
University of Memphis University Singers and The
Glory Gospel Singers of New York. Phylicia works
in various capacities of the music and fine
arts industry as a musician, singer, and educator.
For more information about Phylicia Hollis please
visit: www.phyliciahollisstudios.com.

* 9 7 8 0 6 9 2 8 5 1 4 5 6 *